IRISH
Country
Cooking

IRISH Country Cooking

Helen Walsh

CRESCENT BOOKS
NEW YORK • AVENEL, NEW JERSEY

RECIPES COMPILED BY HELEN WALSH

INTRODUCTION AND CAPTIONS BY ROSAMOND COCKS

FOOD PHOTOGRAPHY BY PETER BARRY

DESIGNED BY PAUL TURNER AND SUE PRESSLEY,

STONECASTLE GRAPHICS LTD

CLB 3243
© 1993 CLB Publishing, Godalming, Surrey, England
All rights reserved
This 1993 edition published by Crescent Books,
distributed by Outlet Book Company, Inc.,
a Random House Company
40 Engelhard Avenue, Avenel, New Jersey 07001

Random House
New York • Toronto • London • Sydney • Auckland

Printed and bound in Singapore by Tien Wah Press
ISBN 0 517 08663 8
8 7 6 5 4 3 2 1

Contents

Introduction
11

Soups & Appetizers
13

Fish & Seafood
31

Meat & Poultry
51

Side Dishes & Snacks
87

Desserts
105

Cakes & Breads
127

Index
140

INTRODUCTION

Water is the key to all things good in Ireland. "The Emerald Isle" lies in the path of predominating south-westerly winds. These warm winds blow in straight off the Atlantic Ocean, and the moisture-laden clouds rise over the coastal hills to give Ireland its high rainfall, 118 inches annually, falling in regular drenching showers, interspersed with sunshine and blue skies. This legendary rainfall gives rise to rich farmland yielding deliciously flavored meats and potatoes. It rarely freezes and seldom gets very hot. Grass is said to grow all year, and the cows and sheep graze greedily. The rains are further significant to the country's cuisine in that they give rise to the sweet groundwater, the primary ingredient for the famous whiskey and Guinness.

Of Ireland's total area, seventy percent is devoted to agriculture and most of the country's farms are devoted to cattle rearing. Beef cattle predominate in central Ireland, while dairy herds predominate in the south. The rearing of sheep, pigs and poultry is common, too. Ireland's country cooking stems from this background of rain and pastureland. Its food is unpretentious and wholesome: meat and potatoes, fish and shellfish from the well-stocked waters, sturdy broths and filling puddings.

The heather-clad hills of Kerry and Wicklow give sweetness to Irish lamb and beef. Irish stew — simply lamb, onion and potatoes — is a deservedly well-known dish, and beef braised in Guinness is a treat as a winter warmer. The rivers and coasts are unpolluted and teeming with life — salmon, salmon trout, mackerel, scallops, mussels and oysters are all delectable in Ireland. Galway is famous for its salmon, and in September it hosts an oyster festival, when every bar in the area serves fresh oysters with soda bread and Guinness. The mussels of Castlemaine Harbour, West Cork and Wexford are huge and succulent and used in many imaginative ways. Waterford and Limerick are renowned for their ham, which for centuries has been a national favorite, perhaps because the potatoes given to the pigs are reputedly so sweet.

Potatoes feature large in the human diet, too, and anyone who has visited Ireland will know how special they are. They are sweeter and nuttier than anywhere else in the world — again, perhaps, thanks to the purity of Ireland's rainwater. Irish potato cakes are a great specialty. Potatoes in Ireland are of special historical interest, too, in that it was the failure of the potato crop due to blight in 1845 that led to devastating famine during the years 1846-1850. It was at this time that 2,000,000 Irish fled the country and imigrated to the shores of the United States.

In the same way that Ireland is permeated with water, so Irish cooking is steeped with their fine and distinctive alcoholic specialties: Guinness, Irish Whiskey, and the liqueur whiskey Irish Mist which is suffused with honey and herbs. Guinness, with its thick, smooth texture and rich, dark flavor marries well with meat and goes into beef stews. The whiskey is used for flaming certain dishes and is found in some cakes. Warming Irish Mist enhances puddings and sweet sauces. The oldest licensed distillery in the world is in Ireland. It lies in the northeast corner of the island in Bushmills, County Antrim. Distilling first began at "Old Bushmills" in 1494, and it became a licensed establishment in 1608. Its whiskey is now world famous, as are many Irish whiskies. The word "whiskey" comes from the Gaelic Uisce beatha, meaning "water of life."

Traveling in Ireland is a delight. Each day gets off to a sustaining start with a wonderful breakfast. Sweet Irish ham or bacon is presented on a giant platter with eggs and soda bread and plenty of butter. Soda bread, a firm tradition and a matter of national pride, is always freshly baked every day. These loaves, baked from stoneground flour, have a lovely hard crust and delicious soft inside.

There are some interesting seasonal dishes in Ireland. For Hallowe'en specialties include Barm Brack, traditionally baked with a ring in it — it is said that whoever finds the ring will be married in the year. There is also Colcannon, a delicate-flavored mixture of hot potato, mashed with cabbage, butter and milk, and seasoned with nutmeg. Dublin Coddle is a third Hallowe'en dish, of bacon, sausages, potatoes and onions. Christmas cake is moistened with whiskey or Guinness, and succulent Irish lamb is traditional at Easter.

A friendly spirit, great hospitality and a love of talk prevails in Ireland, and these attributes, together with the sturdy simple cooking, make eating in Ireland a great occasion every time. Sampling the uncomplicated delights of Irish country cooking outside of Ireland can give one an insight into the ways of rural Ireland and will awaken your taste for the simple good things of life.

SOUPS & APPETIZERS

Mussels in White Wine *page 15*
Dublin Bay Prawn Cocktail *page 16*
Smoked Mackerel Pate *page 19*
Potato Soup *page 20*
Nettle Soup *page 23*
Country Broth *page 24*
Smoked Salmon Bisque *page 27*
Scallops au Gratin *page 28*

14

Mist rises off beautiful Lough Currane, Waterville, a lake famous for its fishing.

Mussels in White Wine

INGREDIENTS
60 mussels
1 large onion, or 4 shallots, finely chopped
½ bottle dry white wine
2 tsps all-purpose flour
2 tsps butter
Salt and pepper
Pinch of ground nutmeg
2 tbsps parsley, chopped

Wash and scrub the mussels well, discarding any that are open. Place in a large saucepan, add the onion or shallots, and wine. Cover and bring to a boil. Cook for about 5 minutes, shaking the saucepan from time to time, or until all the mussels are open. Strain the liquor into another saucepan. Remove the top shells and beards from the mussels and put into warmed soup plates; keep warm. Work the flour into the butter and add the pieces to the strained liquor. Bring to a boil, stirring constantly as it thickens. Season to taste with salt, pepper and nutmeg. Add the parsley and pour over the mussels.

Serves 3-4

Dublin Bay Prawn Cocktail

INGREDIENTS
5-6 lettuce leaves
½ lb cooked, shelled shrimp (frozen shrimp will do)
A little chopped parsley
4 jumbo shrimp
4 lemon wedges for garnish

COCKTAIL SAUCE
2 tbsps tomato paste
1 tsp Worcestershire sauce
2 tsps lemon juice
4 tsps medium sherry
4 heaping tbsps mayonnaise
2 tbsps whipped cream

To make the sauce, add the tomato paste, Worcestershire sauce, lemon juice and sherry to the mayonnaise and mix well. Fold in the whipped cream. Shred the lettuce finely and divide among four glass goblets. If using frozen shrimp, drain them well and place equal amounts of shrimp on top of the lettuce. Just before serving, coat the shrimp with the cocktail sauce and sprinkle a pinch of the chopped parsley on top of each. Garnish with a jumbo shrimp and a lemon wedge on each glass. Serve with buttered brown soda bread.

16

A fishing boat on the Kenmare River,
near Kenmare, County Kerry.

18

Above: the Poulaphouca Reservoir, County Wicklow. Right: the rocky outcrops of the Dingle Peninsula, County Kerry.

Smoked Mackerel Pâté

INGREDIENTS
8 oz skinned, smoked mackerel fillets
⅓ cup softened butter
Juice of 1 lemon
Black pepper
Lemon slices for garnish
Parsley for garnish

This takes only seconds to make in a food processor or electric blender, but if you don't have access to either of these, you can mash up the mackerel in a bowl and thoroughly mix in the butter and lemon juice. Season with freshly ground black pepper and either divide between small individual custard cups or arrange mackerel attractively in a serving dish, garnished with lemon slices and parsley. Serve with brown toast or brown soda bread.

Serves 4

Potato Soup

INGREDIENTS
**2 lbs potatoes
2 onions
1 small carrot
¼ cup butter
5 cups stock
2½ cups milk
Bay leaf, parsley and thyme
Salt and pepper
Cream and chives for garnish**

Peel and slice the potatoes, onions and carrot. Melt butter in a large saucepan and saute the onions in it until soft but not brown. Add potatoes and carrot. Stir in the stock and milk. Tie the bay leaf, thyme and parsley together and add, along with salt and pepper to taste. Simmer gently for about an hour then either blend or put through a sieve or vegetable mill. Add some cream before serving and sprinkle with chopped chives.

Serves 8-10

*Horses are as synonymous with Ireland
as are soda bread and Limerick ham.*

Monaghan, the nearest town to this lovely summer's scene, means "Place of Thickets."

Nettle Soup

INGREDIENTS
2½ cups nettles
¼ cup butter
⅓ cup fine oatmeal
3¾ cups stock
1¼ cups milk

Wear gloves when you are collecting the nettles and only choose the young, bright green leaves. Remove any stalks and chop up the leaves. These days a food processor will do the job in a fraction of the time it takes to chop them by hand. Melt the butter in a large saucepan. Add the oatmeal and cook until the mixture is golden brown. Remove the pan from the heat and add the stock. Bring to a boil and add the milk. When it is boiling again, add the chopped nettles and cook for an additional 4 minutes. You may need more seasoning depending on how much seasoning there is in the stock.

Serves 4

23

Country Broth

INGREDIENTS
1 onion
1 carrot
1 potato
¼ cucumber
½ green pepper
2 tomatoes
Some lettuce leaves
2 stalks celery
2 tbsps oil and 1 tbsp butter
1 handful pearl barley
1 handful macaroni
1 handful lentils
3 pints stock or stock made with bouillon cubes
Some chopped fresh herbs or 1 tsp dried herbs
Salt and pepper
Glass of sherry
2-3 tbsps light cream

Prepare all the vegetables and salad ingredients and chop them roughly. Saute them in the oil and butter, or in butter only, if you prefer. Add the pearl barley, macaroni and lentils then stir in the stock. Add the herbs and seasoning. Bring to the boil and simmer for half an hour. Test for seasoning. If you prefer the soup chunky, mash it down with a potato masher otherwise put it through the coarse shredder of a vegetable mill or a blender. Return it to the pan, add the sherry and the cream or, if necessary, dilute with milk first. Bring back to simmering point and serve.

Serves 8-10

Waiting for the bar to open, Killary Harbour, County Galway.

24

*Killary Harbour, County Galway, is a
10-mile-long fjord-like inlet.*

Smoked Salmon Bisque

INGREDIENTS

Skin and trimmings of a side of smoked salmon
1 carrot
1-2 sticks of celery
1 onion, studded with cloves
Bay leaf
1 tsp salt
Few peppercorns
¼ cup butter
½ cup all-purpose flour
1 tbsp tomato paste
1 glass white wine
4 tbsps cream and 1 tbsp parsley for garnishing

*P*ut the skin and trimmings in a saucepan. Cut the carrot and celery into chunks. Add these to the pan with the onion. Cover with cold water, add the bay leaf, salt and peppercorns. Cover the pan and simmer for about 30 minutes. Remove the bay leaf. Take out the onion, remove the cloves and return the onion to the pan. With a slotted spoon, remove the fish skin and scrape off any remaining flesh, which should also be returned to the pan. Strain half the liquid into a bowl.

In another large pan melt the butter, stir in the flour and make a roux. Stir in the tomato paste and gradually add the strained stock, stirring constantly until it thickens. Add a glass of white wine, or a glass of sherry will do very well! Put the rest of the stock, containing the fish and vegetables, in a blender and run it for half a minute. Add this to the soup. Test for seasoning. You can either stir a spoonful of cream into the soup before serving or put a spoon of cream on top of each bowl. Garnish with a little chopped parsley.

Serves 6-8

Left: sunset over Donegal Bay, which lies near the north end of the Irish west coast where the River Eske flows into the bay.

Scallops au Gratin

INGREDIENTS
2 tbsps oil
¼ cup butter
2-3 tbsps finely chopped shallots (a small onion
   will do)
4 whole scallops
A glass of white wine
2 tbsps heavy cream
2 egg yolks
Salt and pepper
¼ cup grated Cheddar cheese
4 tbsps white bread crumbs

Heat the oil and butter in a heavy frying pan. Add the shallots and cook gently until they soften. Slice the scallop "meat." Raise the heat, stir in the white wine and then the sliced scallops and cook fairly briskly for 2-3 minutes. Slice the bean-like coral of the scallops and add to the pan, cooking the mixture for a further minute.

Mix the cream with the egg yolks and add to the pan. Stir gently over a low heat until the mixture thickens, adding a sprinkling of salt and pepper. Divide between four scallop shells, making sure each one has its fair share of the coral. Place 1 tbsp of grated cheese and 1 tbsp of bread crumbs on each and put under a preheated broiler until just beginning to brown on top. Serve immediately with brown bread.

Serves 4

Above: a horse and trap, like this one in County Kerry, is not an unusual sight in the Irish countryside. Right: massive boulders on the Armagh coast look like beached turtles.

28

FISH & SEAFOOD

Sole Surprise *page 33*
Broiled Trout with Almonds *page 35*
Baked Stuffed Mackerel *page 37*
Poached Salmon Garni *page 38*
Salmon Flan *page 41*
Smoked Salmon Rolls *page 42*
Seafood Pancakes *page 44*
Mackerel Rolls *page 45*
Curried Shrimp Salad *page 46*
Boiled Lobster *page 49*

A little fishing boat near Trench Bridge, Tralee Bay, County Kerry. This area is the gateway to the Dingle Peninsula, a popular base for climbers.

Sole Surprise

INGREDIENTS
8 oz frozen puff pastry
8 oz frozen spinach
¼ cup butter
4 small or 2 large fillets of sole

SAUCE
2 tbsps butter
2 tbsps all-purpose flour
1¼ cups milk
Pinch of fennel
Salt and pepper
½ cup grated cheese

Roll out the thawed pastry into a rectangle 5 x 8 inches. Cut into four equal-size rectangles 2½ x 4 inches. Follow the same procedure for each one. Fold the dough over, short sides together. Cut out the center with a sharp knife, leaving ½ inch all round. Roll out the center piece on a floured board until it is the same size as the ½ inch "frame." Brush the edges with milk and put the "frame" on the base. Brush the top with milk and place on a greased cookie sheet. Bake the pastry in the oven, 425°F, for 10-15 minutes.

Meanwhile, put the spinach in a pan with ¼ inch water and a little salt. Cover and cook for 4-5 minutes. Drain and beat in half the butter. Skin the fillets and, if necessary, cut them in two. Use the rest of the butter to coat two plates and put the fillets on one and cover them with the other. Place the plates over a pan of boiling water and cook for 20 minutes.

For the sauce, melt the butter with the flour to make a roux. Gradually stir in the milk. Bring to a boil. Reduce heat and add seasoning. Cook for another minute, remove from the heat and stir in the cheese.

Divide the spinach between the four pastry boxes. Lay the sole on top and add the sauce.

Serves 4

Broiled Trout with Almonds

INGREDIENTS
4 fresh trout
1 lemon, quartered
¼ cup butter
¼ cup slivered almonds
Parsley for garnish

Clean the trout. Place a lemon wedge in the cavity of each. Line the broiler pan with buttered foil and carefully lay the fish on it. Smear a little butter on each. Preheat the broiler and cook the trout under it for 5 minutes. Turn them very carefully, put a little more butter on top and broil for another five minutes. Keep the fish warm on plates while you toss the almonds in the butter in the broiler pan and brown them under the broiler. Sprinkle them over the fish. Serve with a garnish of lemon slices and parsley.

Serves 4

34

Beautiful spotted trout caught off Ireland's west coast in County Clare, where Europe's highest cliffs are to be found.

This pretty harbor at Kinsale, County Cork, is both a mackerel fishing port and the original home of William Penn, founder of Pennsylvania.

Baked Stuffed Mackerel

INGREDIENTS

1 small onion, finely chopped
¼ cup butter
1 tbsp oatmeal
2 cups bread crumbs
4 mackerel, well cleaned and washed
1 heaping tsp freshly chopped thyme or
**   ½ tsp dried**
1 heaping tsp freshly chopped parsley or
**   ½ tsp dried**
Salt and pepper
2-3 tbsps hot water
1 lemon for garnish

Fry the chopped onion in the butter to soften. Add the oatmeal, bread crumbs, herbs and seasoning. Mix well. Bind with the hot water. Fill the cavities of the fish with the stuffing and wrap each one separately in well-buttered foil. Place in a roasting pan or on a cookie sheet and bake in a pre-heated oven at 375°F, for 25-30 minutes. Serve with lemon slices and thyme.

Serves 4

Poached Salmon Garni

INGREDIENTS
1 fresh whole salmon, approx 2½ lbs, cleaned,
    with head removed
1 tbsp vinegar
1 large lettuce
5-6 hard-boiled eggs
1 lemon, sliced
1 cucumber
3-4 firm tomatoes
Dill for garnish
Mayonnaise

Cut the fish in two, near the gills. Place each piece on a well-buttered piece of foil and make a parcel, folding the top and bottom edges (as well as the side edges) several times. Place the two pieces in a saucepan large enough to hold them side by side, cover them with cold water, add the vinegar and bring slowly to a boil. Gently turn the parcels over in the water. Turn off the heat, cover the pot and leave to cool. Before the fish is completely cold, put the parcels on a large plate, unwrap them and carefully skin and bone the fish. Divide each section into serving-size pieces along the grain of the fish.

Lay the salmon portions in two rows, the length of one or two serving platters, with lettuce leaves between them. Slice the hard-boiled eggs and arrange slices overlapping.

Allow a slice of lemon for each salmon portion and place accordingly. Slice the cucumber and tomatoes and arrange together on the platter. Garnish the salmon with sprigs of dill and serve with mayonnaise.

Serves 8-10

Right: rainclouds roll in onto the rocky Irish coast to water the pastures and feed the rivers.

40

Black Valley, Cummeenduff Glen, County Kerry, offers staggering scenery and excellent fishing.

Salmon Flan

INGREDIENTS
6 oz frozen puff pastry
2 tsps cornstarch
⅔ cup milk
Salt and pepper
6 oz cooked fresh salmon or 7½ oz can of salmon
1 egg, lightly beaten
Dill for garnish

Thaw the pastry. Roll out into a square large enough to line a greased 8-inch flan dish. Trim off the excess pastry and crimp the edges. Mix the cornstarch with 1 tbsp of the milk, bring the rest to a boil, pour into the cornstarch mix, stir well and return to the pan. Return to a boil and cook for 1 minute, stirring constantly. Season well with salt and pepper. If using canned salmon drain the liquid from the can into the sauce. If using fresh salmon add 1 tbsp of butter. Remove the pan from the heat and add the egg, beating it in thoroughly. Flake up the salmon, removing any bones and skin, fold it into the sauce and turn into the pie shell. Bake in the oven, 375°F, for 35-40 minutes. Serve garnished with dill sprigs.

Serves 4-6

Smoked Salmon Rolls

INGREDIENTS
8 oz frozen shrimp
2 tbsps mayonnaise
1 tbsp whipped cream
2 tsps tomato paste
A few drops of lemon juice
8 slices of smoked salmon, about 1 oz each

Thaw shrimp and drain, or use fresh, shelled shrimp instead. Mix mayonnaise, cream, tomato paste and lemon juice in a bowl and fold in shrimp. Divide the mixture between the 8 slices of smoked salmon, placing it on top in a wedge shape and rolling the salmon around it in a cone shape. Allow two per person. Garnish with lemon wedges and sliced cucumber and tomato. Serve with thinly sliced soda bread.

Serves 4

42

It is fun to live in Ireland: the pastures are rich, the rivers and coasts are well stocked with fish, and the roads are quiet enough to ride with a pony and trap.

Seafood Pancakes

INGREDIENTS
1½ lbs fish, trimmed (keep the trimmings)
1 medium onion
Bay leaf
6 peppercorns
1 tsp salt
1 tbsp butter
4 oz mushrooms, sliced
1 tbsp lemon juice in 2 oz water
⅓ tbsp butter
¾ cup all-purpose flour
Glass white wine
2½ cups fish stock
4 oz shrimp (cooked)
Grated nutmeg
⅔ cup whipped cream
12 thin pancakes

Put washed fish trimmings in a pan with the onion, bay leaf, peppercorns, salt and 1 pint water. Bring to a boil and simmer for half an hour. Strain. Cut the fish diagonally into 1-inch strips and poach in the stock for two minutes. Remove fish from the stock and set aside. Melt 1 tbsp of butter in a pan, add the mushrooms, lemon juice and 2 oz water, bring to a boil, reduce heat and cook for 1 minute. Remove mushrooms with a slotted spoon and reserve the stock.

Melt ⅓ cup butter in a saucepan, stir in the flour and cook over low heat for a minute. Add the wine and bring to a boil. Remove pan from heat and slowly add fish and mushroom stocks, stirring all the time. Return to the heat and simmer for 2 minutes. Season with salt and pepper and a little grated nutmeg. Remove from heat and stir in the cream. Use half the sauce to mix in with the fish, shrimp and mushrooms. Divide mixture between the pancakes, roll them up and place side by side in a greased ovenproof dish. Pour over the rest of the sauce and heat in the oven at 350°F for half an hour, or until brown.

Serves 6

Water is the key to all things good in Ireland, most notably the fish, the Guinness and the whiskey.

Mackerel Rolls

INGREDIENTS
4 long, crusty rolls or one loaf French bread
½ tsp thyme, finely chopped
½ tsp mint, finely chopped
Pepper
1 medium apple
1 cup plain yogurt
Few chopped walnuts
12 oz skinned and filleted cooked mackerel

Split rolls or loaf lengthwise. Scoop out some of the center. Chop up bread crumbs on the bread board with two knives. Put the bread crumbs in a bowl and mix in finely chopped herbs and some freshly ground black pepper. Peel, core and quarter the apple; chop it up finely and fold it into the yogurt with the chopped walnuts. Flake the mackerel, mix with the seasoned crumbs and bind with the yogurt mixture. Fill the scooped out rolls with the mixture and either serve as open sandwiches or put tops on and wrap in foil or plastic wrap if using for a picnic. Fill French bread in similar manner and cut into sections.

Serves 4

45

Curried Shrimp Salad

INGREDIENTS
8 oz frozen shrimp
2 tsps tomato paste
A few drops of lemon juice
1 tsp curry powder
4 heaping tbsps mayonnaise
¾ cup cooked rice
Lettuce leaves, hard-boiled egg, cucumber and
    tomato, to garnish

Thoroughly defrost the shrimp. Drain well. Mix tomato paste, lemon juice and curry powder into the mayonnaise. Fold in rice and shrimp. Divide in two and serve on large lettuce leaves. Garnish with sliced, hard-boiled egg, cucumber and tomato.

Serves 4

Farmland at Scrabo Hill, a granite outcrop near the ancient town of Newtownards, County Down.

47

Boiled Lobster

INGREDIENTS
Salt or seaweed
4 1-lb lobsters
Lemon wedges
Parsley sprigs
1 cup melted butter

Fill a large stock pot with water and add salt or a piece of seaweed. Bring the water to a boil and then turn off the heat. Place the live lobsters into the pot, keeping your hand well away from the claws if the claws are not secured. Lower them in claws first. Bring the water slowly back to a boil and cook the lobsters for about 15 minutes, or until they turn bright red. Remove them from the water and drain briefly on paper towels. Place on a plate and garnish with lemon wedges and parsley sprigs. Serve with individual dishes of melted butter for dipping.

Serves 4

Left: a ferry boat in Galway Town, County Galway. Above: a stile looks onto a patchwork of pastures along the Glencree Valley, County Wicklow.

MEAT & POULTRY

Spiced Beef *page 53*
Dublin Coddle *page 54*
Bacon and Egg Pie *page 57*
Irish Stew *page 59*
Crubeens *page 61*
Boiled Ham and Cabbage *page 62*
Limerick Ham *page 65*
Beef Braised in Guinness *page 66*
Sausage Pie *page 69*
Drisheen *page 70*
Tarragon Chicken *page 73*
Boiled Chicken *page 74*
Pheasant in Red Wine *page 77*
Braised Liver and Bacon *page 79*
Marinated Pork Chops *page 81*
Boiled Lamb and Caper Sauce *page 82*
Stuffed Breast of Lamb *page 85*

Beef cattle at Grianan of Aileach, County Donegal, graze the soggy pastures overlooking Lough Swilly.

52

Spiced Beef

INGREDIENTS
3 bay leaves, finely chopped
1 tsp powdered mace
6 finely ground cloves
1 tsp crushed black peppercorns
Large clove garlic made into a paste with salt
1 tsp allspice
2 tbsps molasses
2 heaping tbsps brown sugar
1 lb salt
6 lb piece of brisket, sirloin tip or eye of round

Mix all the spices and flavorings together. Place beef in a large dish and rub well all over with the mixture. Refrigerate in a covered bowl. Repeat this process every day for a week, turning the meat and rubbing in the spices which will now be mixed with the juices drawn from the meat.

Tie the meat up firmly and rub in a final teaspoon of ground cloves. Cover with water and simmer slowly for six hours. When cool enough to handle remove from the cooking liquid, place in a dish and cover with a weighted plate. Slice very thinly and serve.

Serves 6

53

Dublin Coddle

INGREDIENTS
**8 oz thick bacon slices
1 lb pork sausages
1½ lbs potatoes
1 lb onions
Salt and pepper**

Place the bacon and the sausages in a saucepan. Cover with boiling water. Bring back to a boil and simmer for 5 minutes. Drain off the liquid into a bowl and reserve. Peel and slice the potatoes and onions, and place them, with the meat, in a heavy saucepan or greased casserole dish. Cover with the reserved stock, season with salt and pepper before putting on the lid. Simmer on top of the stove of in a moderate oven, 350°F, for about one hour.

Serves 4

Ireland is a country of rolling pastures and rich valleys.

55

56

Above: a lovely view near Kinsale, County Cork. Right: sheep graze the heather-clad hills of the Inishowen Peninsula, County Donegal.

Bacon and Egg Pie

INGREDIENTS
2 cups all-purpose flour
1 tsp salt
⅓ cup margarine
⅓ cup lard or solid shortening
3-4 tbsps cold water
6 slices bacon
6 eggs
Milk for glazing

Sift flour and salt into a bowl. Cut shortening into the flour. Gradually add the water, mixing it in with a knife until the mixture forms a ball and leaves the bowl clean. Lightly shape on a floured board and cut in two. Grease a 10-inch pie plate, roll out half the pastry and line the plate with this. On top of the pastry, arrange the bacon strips like the spokes of a wheel and break an egg into each space. Roll out the other half of the pastry and carefully cover the filling with this. Crimp the edges all round, lightly mark segments with a knife so that each person gets a strip of bacon and an egg, and brush the top with milk. Place in a preheated oven, 400°F, for 40-45 minutes. The pie can be wrapped in layers of newspaper to keep it hot while taking it to a "pot luck" supper, or may be served cold with a salad.

Serves 6

Irish Stew

INGREDIENTS
2 lbs boned lamb or 3 lbs rib chops
2 lbs potatoes
2 large onions
Salt and pepper
1 tbsp fresh, chopped thyme and parsley or
   1 tsp dried thyme
1½ cups water
Chopped parsley for garnish

Trim the meat, leaving a little of the fat on. Peel and slice the potatoes and onions. Season the meat and vegetables with salt, pepper and herbs. Then, starting and finishing with a layer of potatoes, layer the potatoes, meats and onions in a large saucepan or casserole. Add the water and cover tightly. Either simmer on a very low heat on the top of the stove for 2-2½ hours or cook in a slow oven, 275°F, for the same length of time. The pot or casserole should be shaken occasionally to prevent the potatoes from sticking and you should check that the liquid has not dried out. The finished stew should not be too runny, and the potatoes should thicken it enough. Brown the top potato layer under a hot broiler and serve sprinkled with chopped parsley.

Serves 4

58

Grazing sheep have a wild time in County Kerry. The inescapable Irish rain can be seen falling on the hills beyond.

Crubeens

INGREDIENTS
1 pig's trotter (foot) per person
1 onion
1 carrot
Pinch of salt
Few peppercorns
1 bay leaf
Chopped parsley and thyme
Lettuce and tomato for garnish

*P*ut all the ingredients in a pan, cover with cold
water, bring to a boil and simmer for three hours.
Serve surrounded by lettuce and with a tomato
garnish.

Serves 1

*Staying in a Bed and Breakfast in
Ireland, like this in Kerry, is a delight,
not least for the hearty breakfasts of
ham, eggs and soda bread.*

Boiled Ham and Cabbage

INGREDIENTS
Piece of uncooked ham about 3 lbs
1½-2 lbs green cabbage
½ medium-sized onion or one small onion
**   cut in half**

PARSLEY SAUCE
1¼ cups stock
¼ cup butter or margarine
3 tbsps all-purpose flour
1¼ cups milk
½ cup chopped parsley

Soak the ham for several hours or cover it with cold water, bring to a boil, discard water and cover meat with more boiling water. Bring it back to a boil, skim and simmer for 20 minutes to the pound and 20 minutes extra. Reserve the stock.

Meanwhile, cut the cabbage in half and cut out a V in the stalk end of both halves to remove the fibrous end of the stalk. Cut the two halves down through the V and rinse the quarters in salted water. Place in a large saucepan with the cut onion (this miraculously seems to prevent the usual smell of cooked cabbage permeating the house). When the ham is cooked add 3-4 ladles of the stock to the cabbage, cover tightly and cook for about 20 minutes. Meanwhile, skin the ham, cut a lattice pattern in the fat, coat it with brown sugar and stud it with cloves. Brown it in a hot oven while the cabbage is cooking. Drain the cabbage and remove the onion.

Measure out 1¼ cups of the stock in which the cabbage was cooked to use for the parsley sauce. Melt butter or margarine in a saucepan, stir in the flour and make a roux. Cook without browning for a minute or two. Gradually add the stock and then the milk. Bring to a boil and stir for a few minutes. Add the chopped parsley. Adjust the seasoning. Serve with the ham and cabbage and potatoes boiled in their jackets

Serves 6-8

The sheep are barely distinguishable from the rocks, both of which appear strewn over this valley in County Kerry.

63

64

Haymaking and cattle rearing in County Mayo, which, lying in the northwest of the country, gets the country's maximum rainfall.

Limerick Ham

INGREDIENTS
1 smoked ham
1 clove-studded onion
Few peppercorns
1 tbsp honey or brown sugar
Browned bread crumbs (optional)

Soak the ham in water for at least twelve hours, rinse and cover with cold water. Add the clove-studded onion, peppercorns and honey. Bring slowly to a boil, skim, then simmer for 20 minutes per pound plus 20 additional minutes. The ham is cooked when the thick skin peels back easily. Remove the ham from the water and peel off the skin. If it is to be served hot, coat the ham with browned bread crumbs and place it in a roasting pan in the oven, 350°F, for 40 minutes. If it is to be eaten cold it should be put back in the pot after the skin has been removed and allowed to cool in the liquor in which it was cooked. To glaze, heat equal amounts of brown sugar, vinegar and apricot jam, stirring until melted, and then pour the mixture over the ham.

Serves 6

Beef Braised in Guinness

INGREDIENTS
1½ lbs chuck or round roast
2 medium onions
½ lb carrots
2 heaping tbsps all-purpose flour
Salt and pepper
2-3 tbsps cooking oil
½ tsp fresh basil, minced
⅔ cup Guinness
1 tsp honey
⅔ cup stock or water

The roast should be about 1-inch thick and cut into about twelve pieces.

Peel the onions and chop them fairly small. Peel the carrots and slice them into pieces about the size of your little finger. Place the flour in a flat dish and mix in a tsp of salt and a sprinkling of pepper. Heat the oil in the pan, add the onions and cook until soft. Transfer them with a slotted spoon to a large, shallow, greased, ovenproof dish. Dip the pieces of meat in the seasoned flour and brown them in the fat in the pan. Remove these as they are cooked and place in the dish on top of the onions, in a single layer. Arrange the carrots around them. If necessary, add a little more oil to the pan and stir in the remainder of the seasoned flour. Cook for a minute or two, stirring constantly, then add the basil and the Guinness. Allow to boil for a minute or two and then add the honey and the stock. Return to a boil and pour over the meat. Cover the dish either with a lid or with foil and cook in the oven at 325°F for 1½ hours. This dish tastes even better if you cook it the day before and heat it up again in the oven for about 45 minutes. If the gravy looks as though it needs thickening, mix 1 tsp of cornstarch with 2 tbsps of cold water and stir into the gravy 15 minutes before cooking time is up.

Serves 4

Right: a shepherd's cottage on the mountainous Inishowen Peninsula, Donegal, Ireland's most northerly county.

Sausage Pie

INGREDIENTS
¾ lb frozen puff pastry
1 small onion, finely chopped
1 cup bread crumbs
Level tsp dried sage
Salt and pepper
1 lb lean sausage meat
7-oz can tomatoes
1 egg
1 tbsp milk

Cut thawed pastry in two. Roll each half out into a 10-inch square and put it in the refrigerator while you mix the filling. Mix the onion and bread crumbs, herbs and salt and pepper together and mix in with the sausage meat. Add the tomatoes and mix well. Break in the egg and stir that in well. Line a greased 10-inch pie dish with one layer of the pastry. Spread the sausage mixture over it to within 1 inch of the edge. Moisten the edge with milk and place the other piece of pastry on top. Trim the edges and crimp them together all around. Cut a cross in the center on top and use the pastry trimmings to make a leaf pattern in the center. Brush the top with milk and bake in a preheated oven 400°F, for 45 minutes.

Serves 6

Donkeys are one of the many delights of Ireland, symbolizing the country's unhurried way of life.

69

Drisheen

INGREDIENTS
4 cups sheep's blood
2 tsps salt
2½ cups milk
Pinch thyme
2 cups bread crumbs
Lettuce and tomato for garnish

*Strain the blood into a mixing bowl, add all the
other ingredients and mix well. Let stand for half
an hour, then pour mixture into a greased
ovenproof dish. Cover with foil and place in a
roasting pan with enough water to come halfway
up the sides of the dish. Bake in the oven at 350°F
for 45 minutes or until set. Serve garnished with
lettuce and tomato.*

Serves 8

These lovely curly-horned sheep in Kerry are a common sight all over Ireland.

71

72

Domestic fowl take the air, backed by The Twelve Bens rising in their quarzite conical peaks behind Lough Inagh.

Tarragon Chicken

INGREDIENTS
3½ lbs chicken with giblets
Salt and pepper
Tarragon
1 onion, quartered
1 carrot, quartered
1 stick celery, quartered
1 bay leaf

SAUCE
¼ cup butter
½ cup all-purpose flour
Glass white wine or cider
1 tsp chopped tarragon
2 tsps chopped parsley
Juice of ½ lemon
3 heaping tbsps whipped cream
3 heaping tbsps mayonnaise

Sprinkle the inside of the chicken with salt, pepper and tarragon. Place the onion, carrot, celery and bay leaf in a pan just large enough to hold the chicken. Add giblets. Place the chicken on top and pour over enough water just to cover. Cover the pan tightly and bring to a boil. Reduce heat and simmer for 1 hour. Remove pan from the heat and turn the chicken breast-side down in the stock, being careful not to break the skin. Cover and allow to cool. This can be done the day before. Skin the chicken and slice meat from the bones.

Melt the butter in a heavy saucepan. Stir in the flour and cook for a minute or two. Add the wine or cider. Gradually stir in the stock. Add the tarragon, parsley and lemon juice and bring sauce to a boil. Cook for another 2 minutes, stirring constantly. Remove from heat and allow to cool before folding in the cream and the mayonnaise.

Toss the chicken pieces in about ¾ of the sauce and pile them into a large, shallow serving dish. Coat with the remainder of the sauce and garnish with tarragon sprigs and strips of lemon rind before serving.

Serves 6-8

Boiled Chicken

INGREDIENTS
2-3 oz chicken fat
1 large boiling fowl
Salt and pepper
1 onion, chopped
1 carrot, chopped
1 turnip, chopped
1 stick celery, chopped
A bouquet garni

PARSLEY SAUCE
¼ cup butter
½ cup all-purpose flour
1¼ cups stock
1¼ cups milk
Cupful of chopped parsley
Salt and pepper

Put 2-3 oz of chicken fat in a large pan. Wash and dry the bird, inside and out, and season well with salt and pepper. Brown slightly in the fat, remove the chicken and add the vegetables. Turn them in the fat for a few minutes then add the chicken and cover with boiling water. Add salt, pepper and bouquet garni. Bring back to a boil, skim, then cover the pot and simmer the contents slowly for about three hours or 40 minutes to the pound.

When the bird is cooked, remove it from the pot and keep hot on a serving dish. Melt the butter in a saucepan, stir in the flour and cook for a minute. Remove from heat and gradually stir in 1¼ cups of the strained chicken stock. Return to the heat and, when it has thickened, gradually add the milk and continue cooking until it boils again. Lower the heat and cook for another 2 minutes; add parsley and season with salt and pepper. Serve separately in a gravy boat.

Serves 4-6

Right: the sun setting over the County Londonderry coast.

Good hunting country in Tipperary. The name became familiar during the First World War when British Troops sang "It's a long way to Tipperary."

Pheasant in Red Wine

INGREDIENTS
2 tbsps oil
1 tbsp butter
1 large pheasant
2 eating apples
1 onion
4 tsps all-purpose flour
⅔ cup stock or water
⅔ cup red wine
Rind and juice of 1 orange
1 heaping tsp brown sugar
Salt and pepper
Bay leaf, sprig of parsley and thyme,
    tied together

Preheat the oven to 350°F. Melt the oil and butter in a heavy pan. Add the pheasant, turning it to brown all over, then remove and place it in a casserole dish with the apples. Chop the onion and add it to the fat in the pan. Allow it to soften without browning. Stir in the flour then gradually add the stock and the wine and bring to a boil, stirring constantly. Add the grated orange rind, the orange juice and the sugar. Season with salt and pepper and pour the sauce over the pheasant. Add the herbs, cover the casserole and bake in the preheated oven for one hour.

Serves 4

77

Braised Liver and Bacon

INGREDIENTS
1 large onion
3 tbsps oil
8 slices of lamb's liver
3 tbsps all-purpose flour seasoned with salt and pepper
1 glass of red wine
14-oz can chopped tomatoes
1 heaping tsp honey
½ tsp dried basil
4 thick slices of bacon
3 cups pasta shells or macaroni

Peel and slice the onion. Heat oil in a frying pan and fry the onion until soft. Transfer onion with a slotted spoon to an ovenproof dish large enough to take all the liver in one layer. Dredge liver in seasoned flour, brown lightly in remaining oil in frying pan and lay on top of onions. Mix remainder of seasoned flour with pan juices and mix to a paste over low heat. Add red wine and bring to the boil. Remove 2 tbsps of the chopped tomatoes and reserve, add the rest to the pan with the honey and basil. Bring mixture to a boil, stirring well. Pour around the liver in the dish. Slice bacon in half and place on top of liver. Put dish in a preheated oven at 375°F for about 20 minutes.

Cook pasta shells or macaroni in boiling, salted water, following instructions on packet. Drain. Heat remaining tomatoes in a saucepan with a pinch of basil. Toss pasta in it and transfer to a serving dish to accompany the liver and bacon.

Serves 4

Above: a peat cutter and his dog, County Kerry. Right: rock outcrops and spring flowers color the hills of Cork, Ireland's most southerly county.

Marinated Pork Chops

INGREDIENTS
4 pork chops
1 onion, finely chopped
½ tsp sage
½ tsp thyme
1 cup cider
2 tbsps oil
1 tbsp butter
½ cup flour, seasoned with salt and pepper
1 or 2 apples, peeled, cored and sliced
¾ cup stock
1 tsp honey
1 tsp Dijon mustard

Place the chops in a shallow ovenproof dish just large enough to hold them. Add the onion and herbs to the cider and pour over the chops. Leave for several hours, turning the meat occasionally. Heat the oil and butter in a frying pan. Drain the chops and dredge them in the seasoned flour, lightly coating both sides. Seal them in the frying pan, browning them slightly. Strain the marinade into a bowl. Wash and grease the baking dish. Layer the sliced apple on the bottom and place the chops on top. Add the onion from the marinade to the fat in the frying pan. Cook until soft and stir in the remainder of the seasoned flour. Allow it to brown, stirring constantly, then gradually add the liquid from the marinade and the stock. Stir in the honey and the mustard, bring to a boil and pour over the chops. Cover with foil and cook in a preheated oven, 350°F, for 45 minutes. Serve with peas and creamed potatoes.

Serves 4

Left: a horse-drawn outing in County Kerry.

Boiled Lamb and Caper Sauce

INGREDIENTS
10 lb leg of lamb
CAPER SAUCE
¼ cup butter or dripping
½ cup all-purpose flour
1¼ cups milk
1¼ cups pot liquor
Salt and pepper
1 heaping tbsp capers and a little of their
preserving liquid

*To boil a leg of lamb, allow 20 minutes to the
pound and 20 minutes extra. Plunge the joint into
enough boiling, salted water to cover it and boil
for 4-5 minutes, then reduce the heat and simmer
gently for the remainder of the cooking time.*

*For the caper sauce, melt the butter in a heavy
pan, stir in the flour and cook for a minute but do
not allow to brown. Remove from heat and stir in
a little of the milk, then gradually add rest of the
milk over gentle heat, stirring all the time.
Gradually add 1 cup of the hot cooking liquor
and bring to a boil. Boil for 2-3 minutes, stirring
constantly. Test for flavor and season with pepper
and more salt, if necessary. If it seems of a good
coating consistency, add the capers and a little of
the preserving liquid but do not bring the sauce
back to a boil or it will curdle.*

*Pour a little of the sauce over the joint and
serve the remainder separately. Serve with boiled
white turnips and parsnips and garnish with
parsley.*

Serves 8-10

Left: sheep shearing in County Galway, on Ireland's west coast. Above: sheep grazing in the shade are backed by Ireland's gorgeous late summer colors.

Horned sheep graze greedily in County Kerry, on this "Emerald Isle."

84

Stuffed Breast of Lamb

INGREDIENTS
Half breast of lamb
1 medium onion
Salt and pepper
4 cups white bread crumbs
¼ cup chopped lard
½ tsp marjoram
½ tsp thyme
Grated rind of half a lemon
1 egg
1 tbsp all-purpose flour

Bone the breast of lamb with a sharp knife. Place the bones in a saucepan with half the onion and some salt and pepper. Cover with water, bring to a boil, skim, cover the pot and simmer for half an hour.

Mix the bread crumbs, lard, herbs, lemon rind, a little salt and pepper and the other half of the onion, minced, and the egg. Add 2-3 tbsps of the bone stock and spread the stuffing on the breast of lamb. Roll up, starting at the wide end. Tie up firmly with string and place in a greased roasting pan. Bake in the oven, 400°F, for 1 hour.

Transfer the meat to a serving dish and keep hot while you make the gravy. Drain off any excess fat from the roasting pan, retaining about two tablespoons. Stir in the flour and heat on the stove until mixture browns. Stir in about a cupful of the stock. Bring to a boil, stirring constantly. Boil for a few minutes and then strain into a gravy boat and serve with the stuffed lamb. Serve with new potatoes and zucchini.

Serves 4

SIDE DISHES & SNACKS

Colcannon *page 89*
Stuffed Summer Squash *page 90*
Champ *page 92*
Stuffed Grape Leaves *page 93*
Dulse *page 94*
Mushrooms on Toast *page 96*
Irish Rarebit *page 97*
Boxty Pancakes *page 98*
Potato Cakes *page 101*
Oaten Farls *page 102*
Flummery *page 103*

The rock of Dunamase, County Laois, is a 200-foot-high fort, or dun, first occupied by a Leinster chieftain in early Christian times.

Colcannon

INGREDIENTS
½ cup finely chopped onion, leek or scallion
¼ cup butter
¼ cup milk
1 lb cooked mashed potatoes
1½ cups cooked cabbage

Gently fry the onion in melted butter until soft. Add the milk and the well-mashed potatoes and stir until heated through. Chop the cabbage finely and beat into the mixture over a low heat until all the mixture is pale green and fluffy. This dish is an excellent accompaniment for boiled ham.

Serves 4

Stuffed Summer Squash

INGREDIENTS
6-8 oz cooked lamb
1 onion
1 carrot
1 cup of gravy or stock made with bouillon cube
3 large tomatoes or 7-oz can of tomatoes, drained
1-2 cups cooked rice, according to the size of the
squash
½ tsp oregano plus chopped mixed garden herbs
if available
Salt and pepper
1 large summer squash
1 cup grated cheese

Put the lamb, onion and carrot through the grinder or chop in food processor. Mix in a bowl with the gravy or stock. Put tomatoes in boiling water and let stand for a few minutes then remove skins, chop the pulp and add to mixture. If using canned tomatoes, drain off liquid, chop up tomatoes and add to mixture. Add rice and herbs and season with salt and pepper to taste. Scrub squash well. Cut in half lengthwise, remove seeds and fill both halves with stuffing. Place side by side in a greased roasting pan with about half an inch of water in it. Cover pan with foil and bake at 400°F for one hour. Remove from oven, take off foil, sprinkle grated cheese over squash and return to oven for an additional ten minutes.

Serves 4-6

Right: these horned sheep are well suited to the rough grazing to be had in the country's rugged hills.

Champ

INGREDIENTS
1½ lbs cooked potatoes
4 oz scallions
½ cup milk
Salt and pepper
4 large pats butter

Peel the potatoes and boil them in salted water. Drain them well and allow to dry out completely. Meanwhile, trim and wash the scallions. Slice them finely, including the green part, and put them in a saucepan with the milk to simmer gently until soft. Drain the scallions, reserving the milk, and beat them into the potato, gradually adding the hot milk until you have a nice fluffy mixture. Season well with salt and pepper and divide between four bowls, shaping each serving into a mound with a dent in the top into which you put the butter. It is eaten by dipping the potato into the melted butter.

Serves 4

It is the constant interchange between sun and rain that gives Ireland its rich pastures.

Stuffed Grape Leaves

INGREDIENTS
2-3 scallions, finely chopped
2-3 tbsps oil
4 oz cold lamb, ground
8 oz cooked rice
½ tsp marjoram
1 tbsp finely chopped walnuts
Salt and pepper
24 grape leaves
1¼ cups stock
Lemon wedges for garnish

Fry the scallions in the oil then add the lamb, rice, marjoram and walnuts. Season with salt and pepper. Have ready a pan of boiling water and a bowl of iced water. Hold the grape leaves by their stalks and dip each one into the boiling water for about 10 seconds then plunge it into the iced water. Lay the leaves, underside up, on a board and put a tsp of the filling on each. Roll each one up into a sausage shape, tucking in the edges, and gently squeeze into shape in the palm of your hand. Pack the little parcels into a large pan in one layer. Pour the stock over them and cover with a plate to keep them in position. Simmer for half an hour, and serve with wedges of lemon.

Serves 8

Glencar Waterfall lies at the eastern end of two-mile-long Glencar Lough, County Sligo.

Dulse

Seaweed has been popular in Ireland for centuries, and its salty, tangy flavor blends particularly well with potatoes. Dulse is a dried form of seaweed, and is usually eaten raw. It is often used instead of scallions to make Champ. When cooked, it must first be soaked for several hours. A similar seaweed, Carrigeen, is also popular in Ireland, and is found along America's Atlantic coastline, too.

Above and right: fishing boats in Waterford Harbour, in the southeast of the country.

Mushrooms on Toast

INGREDIENTS

**8 oz freshly gathered field mushrooms, or use the
large, flat, cultivated variety**
2½ cups milk
¼ cup butter
¼ cup all-purpose flour
Salt and pepper

*Wipe mushrooms with damp paper towels. Slice
and place in a pan with the milk. Bring slowly to
a boil and simmer gently for ten minutes.
Meanwhile, melt butter in another pan, add flour
and stir. Cook over very low heat for about a
minute. Strain the milk in which the mushrooms
were cooked into a container and gradually add it
to the roux, stirring all the time. When the sauce
has thickened add the mushrooms, season with
salt and pepper and serve on buttered toast.*

Serves 4-6

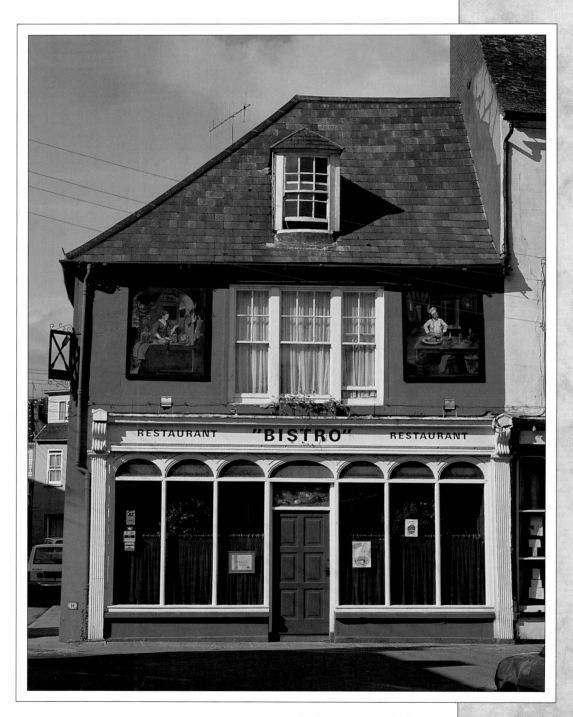

*An elegant restaurant in the
picturesque and historic town of
Kinsale, County Cork.*

Irish Rarebit

INGREDIENTS

2 tbsps butter or margarine
2 tbsps all-purpose flour
½ cup milk
1 tsp Dijon mustard
1 tsp honey
½ cup Guinness
1 cup Cheddar cheese, grated
Salt and pepper

Melt the butter in a heavy pan and stir in the flour to make a roux. Cook on a low heat for a further minute without allowing the roux to brown. Remove pan from heat and gradually beat the milk into the roux. Return to heat and stir until the mixture thickens. Stir in mustard and honey and finally the Guinness. Cook this mixture fairly rapidly for 2-3 minutes then add grated cheese and stir over very low heat only until all the cheese has melted. Spread thickly on four slices of toast and brown under the broiler.

Serves 4

Boxty Pancakes

INGREDIENTS
½ lb raw potatoes
8 oz mashed potatoes
1 tsp salt
1 tsp baking soda
2 cups all-purpose flour
Pepper
¼ cup butter, margarine or bacon fat
Milk

Peel and grate the raw potatoes. Wrap them tightly in a cloth and squeeze over a bowl to extract as much of the starch liquid as possible. Thoroughly blend the grated raw potato into the cooked mashed potato. Pour the liquid off the bowl of potato starch and scrape the starch into the potato mixture. Sift the salt and baking soda with the flour and add to the potatoes, mix well. Add the melted fat and mix again. Add as much milk as necessary to make the mixture into a batter of dropping consistency, season with pepper and cook in spoonfuls on a greased griddle or heavy pan until crispy and golden on both sides.

Serves 6

Gorse in bloom near Hollywood,
County Wicklow, on the edge of the
Wicklow Mountains.

Straw bales, backed by untouched Irish upland.

Potato Cakes

INGREDIENTS
1 cup all-purpose flour
½ tsp salt
½ tsp baking powder
2 tbsps butter
2¾ cups mashed potato
Bacon fat or dripping

Sift flour, salt and baking powder. Cut in the butter. Mix in the potatoes and knead into a ball. Cut this in two and roll half out on a floured board or work surface into a circle half an inch thick. Divide into four segments. Cook them for 2-3 minutes each side, on a very hot pan or griddle greased with bacon fat or dripping. Repeat the process with the other half.

Serves 8

Oaten Farls

In the north of Ireland, the nearer one gets to the coast of Scotland, the more the Scottish influence is noticed in the food, and many recipes in this part of Ireland contain oatmeal. Here is one for potato cakes mixed with oatmeal.

Make the potato cakes as in the recipe, but before rolling out knead a handful of oatmeal into each half. Sprinkle the board with more oatmeal and roll out the potato mixture, turning it over so that both sides are well coated. Divide into farls and cook in a little fat on a heavy frying pan or griddle.

Flummery

A boulder-strewn river meanders
through woodland in Tipperary.

<u>INGREDIENTS</u>
2 cups oatmeal
5 cups water
½ tsp salt

Oatmeal was sometimes used to make gruel – the thinnest imaginable mixture of oatmeal and water, or milk and water. There was just about enough nourishment in it to keep people alive during the famine – the lucky ones that is! Flummery is a more substantial version of this, and it was traditionally given to children and to invalids.

Soak the oatmeal in the water for at least 24 hours. Strain through cheesecloth, and boil the liquid for 20-30 minutes, stirring all the time. Add salt and serve with milk or cream.

Serves 4-6

103

DESSERTS

Almond Tart *page 107*
Bananas with Irish Mist *page 108*
Tipsy Cake *page 111*
Apple Cake *page 112*
Rhubarb Fool *page 115*
Bread and Butter Pudding *page 116*
Summer Pudding *page 119*
Queen of Puddings *page 120*
Baked Custard *page 121*
Raspberry Souffle *page 122*
Carrigeen Moss Pudding *page 125*

Beef cattle enjoy the buttercups and daisies overlooking this gorgeous Cork beach, or "strand."

Almond Tart

INGREDIENTS
6 oz frozen puff pastry
½ cup butter or margarine
½ cup superfine sugar
2 eggs
1 tsp baking powder
½ tsp almond extract
1 cup all-purpose flour, sifted
2½ tsps milk
Damson jam
¼ cup grated almond paste (left uncovered in the refrigerator to harden before grating)

Take ⅔ of the puff pastry, roll it out thinly and line a greased 10-inch tart pan with it, allowing a 1-inch overlap all round. Roll out the remainder of the pastry slightly thicker, cut into strips ½-inch wide and set aside.

Cream the slightly softened butter or margarine and sugar together. Add eggs one at a time, beating well. Before adding the second egg, beat in 1 tbsp of the sifted flour. Mix the almond extract with the milk, add to the mixture then fold in the remainder of the flour and the baking powder.

Spread the jam on the pastry to within 1 inch of the rim. Sprinkle with the grated almond paste on top. Cover with the sponge mixture using a spatula, being careful not to disturb the filling. Make a lattice with the pastry strips over the top and crimp the edges, turning in the overlap of pastry to form a rim.

Bake in the oven at 400°F for 20 minutes, then 350°F for another 15 minutes.

Serves 8-10

107

Bananas with Irish Mist

INGREDIENTS
¼ cup butter
4 bananas
4 tsps superfine sugar
4 tsps Irish Mist (whiskey liqueur)

Melt the butter in a heavy frying pan. Peel the bananas and place them whole in the pan, turning them carefully in the melted butter. Cook them over a low heat for about 3 minutes on each side until they are heated through. Place them on individual plates and keep them warm while you make the sauce. Add the superfine sugar to the remaining butter in the pan. Stir over a low heat until dissolved. Add the Irish Mist, stir well and bring the mixture to a boil. Slice the hot bananas and then spoon the sauce over them.

Serves 4

Looking deceptively similar to the national drink, the peat-stained waters of this Irish river course through cool woods.

Tipsy Cake

INGREDIENTS
14-oz can fruit cocktail
¼ cup sherry
2 oz amaretti
About 16 ladyfingers
Raspberry jam
2 oz slivered almonds

CUSTARD
2 level tbsps cornstarch
1 oz vanilla sugar (or sugar and ½ tsp vanilla
**   extract)**
1¼ cups milk
1 tbsp sherry
1 egg
1¼ cups whipped cream, not too stiff
Few candied cherries, halved

Drain the fruit cocktail into bowl. Measure out ¼ of the juice and add the sherry. Crumble the amaretti, saving some for decoration. Spread the ladyfingers with raspberry jam and use to line the bottom of a glass serving bowl. Place half the fruit on top and sprinkle with some amaretti and slivered almonds and ⅓ of the juice and sherry mixture. Repeat this once, then cover with the final layer of ladyfingers and add the rest of the juice.

Place the cornstarch and sugar in a small mixing bowl, mix with 2 tbsps of the milk, bring the rest of the milk to a bowl. Pour it over the cornstarch mixture, stirring constantly. Return the pan to the heat and bring the custard back to a boil and simmer for 1 minute. Remove from the heat and beat in the tablespoonful of sherry and the lightly beaten eggs. Cool and, while lukewarm, pour over the ladyfingers. Chill thoroughly. To serve, top with whipped cream and decorate with the amaretti and cherries.

Serves 8

Left: donkey and trap in Collooney, County Sligo. This is still a common sight all over Ireland.

Apple Cake

INGREDIENTS
1 tsp cinnamon
1½ cups self-rising flour
¾ cup butter or margarine
¾ cup superfine sugar
3 eggs
2 tbsps milk
2-3 eating apples, peeled, cored and thinly sliced

Add the cinnamon to the flour and sift into a bowl. Cream butter and sugar until light and soft. Beat in one egg then add a tbsp of the flour and beat in another egg. Repeat this once more then fold in two-thirds of the remaining flour. Stir in the milk, then fold in the last of the flour. Grease either a lasagne dish or a roasting pan approx. 11 x 8½ inches. Spread half the batter in the bottom, distribute the apple slices over it and cover with the rest of the batter. Bake in the oven at 350°F for 15 minutes and reduce heat to 325°F. Continue baking for 30 minutes until golden brown and firm to the touch.

112

Peaceful grazing cattle on the banks of
Lough Gur, County Limerick.

113

A view from the hills of Kerry down to the coast.

Rhubarb Fool

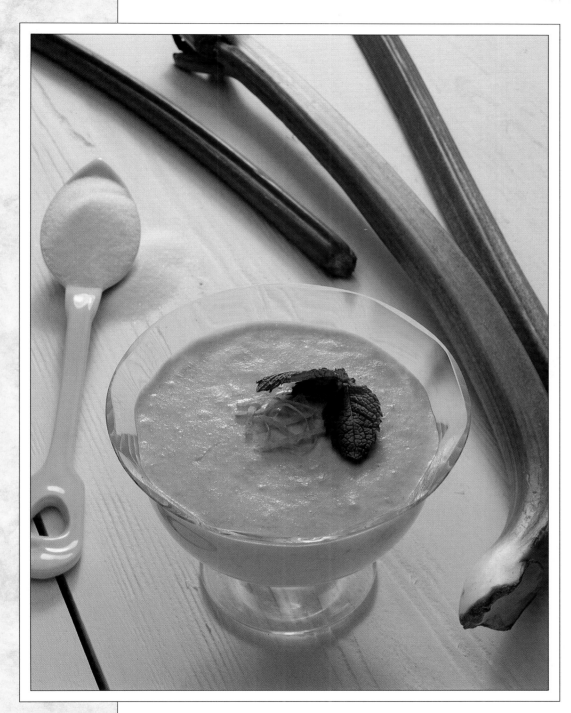

INGREDIENTS
1 lb rhubarb
¼ cup sugar
2-3 strips of lemon rind
1¼ cups whipped cream
Lemon rind and mint to decorate

Trim and scrub the rhubarb and cut into 1-inch lengths. Be careful to remove all trace of the leaves, which are poisonous. Place in a buttered ovenproof dish with a lid. Add sugar, lemon rind and about 3 tbsps water. Cover and cook in a slow oven, 300°F, for about 40 minutes or until the rhubarb is soft. Purée in a blender and allow to cool before folding in the whipped cream. Chill before serving. Decorate with strips of lemon rind and mint leaves.

Serves 6

Bread and Butter Pudding

INGREDIENTS
Butter or margarine
4-5 slices of bread from a medium-sliced loaf
¾ cup sugar with 1 tsp cinnamon mixed in
   ½ cup golden raisins
2 cups milk
2 eggs

Butter the bread and cut into triangles. Grease a 3-4 cup ovenproof dish and put in layers of bread, sugar and raisins. Heat the milk and pour over the beaten eggs. Pour mixture over bread and fruit. Bake for 40-45 minutes at 350°F.

Serves 6

Right: straw bales backed by conical hills on the Cooley Peninsula, County Louth.

116

Summer Pudding

INGREDIENTS
Unsliced loaf of bread
1½ lbs fruit (raspberries, redcurrants or blackberries)
½ cup sugar

Line a pudding bowl with bread as follows. Cut some slices of bread about half an inch in thickness. From one of these cut a round to fit easily in the bottom of the bowl. For the sides cut the bread in finger pieces, the height of the bowl in length, and, in breadth, about one and a half inches at one end and one inch at the other. Pack these tightly around the sides of the bowl.

   Stew the fruit, adding sugar to taste, and if not very juicy add a little water. While hot, pour into the lined bowl and cover the top with bread. Set it on a plate so as to catch any juice that may flow over. Place a small plate on top of the bread and over this a weight. When cold, turn out and pour around it any juice that may have run into the plate. Serve with custard, cream or milk.

Serves 8

Left: a beached fishing boat looks down on to the choppy waters of Dingle, County Kerry.

Queen of Puddings

INGREDIENTS
1½ cups milk
2 tbsps butter
3 medium slices of white bread, crusts removed
Grated rind of 1 lemon
1 tbsp sugar
2 eggs
2 tbsps red jelly
Heaping tbsp sugar

Heat the milk with the butter. When simmering, remove the pan from the heat and add the bread, lemon rind and sugar. Allow to stand for 10-15 minutes then beat the mixture until no lumps remain. Separate the eggs and beat the yolks into the mixture. Grease a 3-4 cup ovenproof glass dish and pour the mixture into it. Bake in a moderate oven, 350°F, until it is set – about 25 minutes. Spread the jelly gently over the top, being careful not to break the surface. Whisk the egg whites until stiff, add the heaping tablespoon sugar and whisk again. Spoon the meringue over the pudding, making sure to cover the pudding right up to the edges and lifting the spoon to form little peaks. Return the dish to the oven for about 10 minutes until the "peaks" are golden brown.

Serves 4-6

Baked Custard

INGREDIENTS
2 eggs
2 tbsps sugar
2½ cups milk
Grated nutmeg

Beat the eggs with the sugar in a mixing bowl. Heat the milk but do not let it boil. Pour it slowly onto the egg and sugar mixture, stirring all the time. Pour the mixture into a greased ovenproof dish or casserole and grate nutmeg over the top. Place the dish in a roasting pan containing about 1 inch of warm water and bake in the oven for 45 minutes at 325°F.

Serves 4

A "Jaunting car" rolls along the shores of Muckross Lough, County Kerry, in the grounds of Muckross House.

121

Raspberry Soufflé

INGREDIENTS
**1 lb raspberries (frozen raspberries, thawed,
    can be used)**
½ cup superfine sugar
1 envelope gelatin
4 eggs, separated
¼ cup confectioners' sugar
1¼ cups heavy cream, lightly whipped
Mint sprigs to decorate

*Tie a greased piece of wax paper around a 6-inch
soufflé dish to form a collar above the rim of the
dish. Reserve a few of the raspberries and strain
the rest. Fold the superfine sugar into the purée.
Soften the gelatin in half a cup of cold water, then
heat over a pan of hot water until it has dissolved
completely. Allow it to cool a little. Whisk the egg
yolks and sugar together over the hot water. Fold
in the raspberry purée and the gelatin and cool.
Fold in half the cream. Whisk the egg whites until
stiff, and fold into the mixture with a metal spoon.
Turn into the prepared soufflé dish and leave to
set. When set, remove the collar carefully and
decorate the soufflé with the remaining whipped
cream, raspberries and mint sprigs.*

Serves 6

A patchwork quilt of farmland viewed from the Rock of Dunamase, the ancient 200-foot-high fort ruins in County Laois.

124

Above: the rolling hills of County Cork are the natural habitat for sure-footed sheep. Right: a diet of wild flowers and lush grass gives good milk.

Carrigeen Moss Pudding

INGREDIENTS
Approx ¼ oz Carrigeen moss
2 cups milk
Grated rind of ½ lemon
2 tbsps sugar

Take as much Carrigeen as will fit in your fist when almost clenched. Wash it in warm water for a few minutes, removing any grasses or other foreign bodies. Place the moss in a pan with the milk, grated lemon rind and sugar. Bring slowly to the boil and simmer gently for 15-20 minutes. String through a sieve, being sure to scrape all the jelly into the bowl. Stir well and transfer the mixture into a wet mold or serving bowl. Let it set in a cool place overnight or for several hours before turning out onto a serving dish. Serve with cream and strawberry or raspberry jam.

Serves 6

CAKES & BREADS

Guinness Cake *page 129*
Barm Brack *page 130*
Irish Coffee Cake *page 133*
Golden Raisin Soda Bread *page 134*
Irish Soda Bread *page 137*
Yellow Man *page 138*

Irish bars are not fancy, but the warmth of your welcome, the flavor of your drink, and the smoldering peat fire are a delight to encounter

Guinness Cake

INGREDIENTS
1 cup butter or margarine
1 cup brown sugar
1¼ cups Guinness
1½ cups raisins
1½ cups currants
1½ cups golden raisins
¾ cup shredded orange and lemon peel, mixed
5 cups all-purpose flour
1 tsp allspice
1 tsp nutmeg
½ tsp baking soda
3 eggs

Grease and line a 9-inch cake pan with wax paper. Place the butter, sugar and the Guinness in a saucepan and bring slowly to a boil, stirring constantly until the sugar and butter have melted. Mix in the dried fruit and peel and bring the mixture back to a boil. Simmer for 5 minutes. Remove from the heat and cook thoroughly. Sift the flour, spice and baking soda into a large mixing bowl. Stir in the cooled fruit mixture and beaten eggs. Turn into the cake pan and bake in the center of a pre-heated oven, 325°F for 2 hours. Test with a skewer. When done, cool in the pan before removing the cake.

Barm Brack

INGREDIENTS
½ tsp salt
½ tsp cinnamon
Pinch grated nutmeg
4 cups all-purpose flour
¼ cup softened butter
⅓ cup superfine sugar
1 cup milk, at room temperature
1 package active dry yeast
1 egg
1¼ cups golden raisins
1 cup currants
½ cup shredded orange and lemon peel, mixed

Add the salt and spices to the flour and sift into a large mixing bowl. Cut in the butter. Add a tsp of the sugar and a tsp of the milk to the yeast and mix well. Add the remainder of the sugar to the flour mixture and mix in. Lightly beat the egg, add the milk, and pour this into the yeast mixture. Add this to the flour and beat very well by hand, or in a mixer fitted with a dough hook, until the batter becomes stiff and elastic. Fold in the raisins, currants and shredded peel and cover the bowl with lightly greased plastic wrap. Leave the bowl in a warm place for 1-2 hours, to allow the dough to rise. Divide the mixture between two greased loaf pans 8½ x 4½-inch, or two 7-inch cake pans. Cover again and allow to rise for half an hour. Bake for one hour in center of oven at 375°F. Dissolve a tbsp of sugar in a quarter cup of hot water and brush over brack, return it to the oven for five minutes with the heat turned off. Turn out onto a rack to cool. Slice and butter.

Of Ireland's total area, seventy percent is devoted to agriculture, which makes for stunning scenery, as here in County Laois.

131

Irish Coffee Cake

INGREDIENTS
½ cup butter or margarine
½ cup superfine sugar
2 eggs
1 cup all-purpose flour
1 tsp baking powder
2 tsps instant coffee dissolved in 2 tbsps hot water

SYRUP
½ cup sugar
⅔ cup strong coffee
3 tbsps Irish whiskey

TOPPING
⅔ cup whipping cream
1 heaping tbsp confectioners' sugar
1 tbsp Irish whiskey
Whole hazelnuts

Grease an 8-inch ring pan and coat well with flour. In a bowl, cream together the butter and sugar, then add the eggs one at a time. Sift the flour and baking powder and fold ⅔ of it into the mixture. Add the 2 tbsps strong coffee. Mix well. Fold in the remainder of the flour. Place in the prepared cake pan and bake in a pre-heated oven at 350°F for 35-40 minutes. Test with a skewer and when done, turn out onto a wire rack to cool.

To make the syrup: heat sugar in coffee until dissolved, then boil rapidly for 1 minute. Remove from the heat and beat in the whiskey. Return the cooled cake to the well-washed pan and pour the syrup over it. Let it soak for several hours. Beat the cream with confectioners' sugar and whiskey. Turn the cake out onto a serving plate and decorate with cream and whole hazelnuts. Chill before serving.

Golden Raisin Soda Bread

INGREDIENTS
4 cups white, all-purpose flour
1 tsp salt
1 tsp baking soda
1 tsp cream of tartar
1 level tbsp sugar
⅔ cup golden raisins
1¼ cups sour milk or fresh milk with 1 tbsp
    yogurt mixed in

Sift flour, salt, baking soda and cream of tartar into a mixing bowl. Stir in sugar and golden raisins then add the milk, mixing to form a firm, but not too stiff, dough. Knead lightly on a floured board and form into a slightly flattened round. Cut a deep cross on the top and brush the top with milk. Place on a greased, lightly floured cookie sheet and bake in the center of the oven at 400°F for 25 minutes. Turn the loaf upside down on the tray and return to oven for another five minutes. The loaf is done when it sounds hollow when tapped on the base. Wrap in a damp cloth and place on its side to cool.

This glorious gorse is in County Louth, which lies on the Irish east coast near the border with Northern Ireland.

135

Although most agricultural land is given over to pasture land, cereals are an important part of the Irish economy, too.

Irish Soda Bread

INGREDIENTS
1 tsp salt
1 tsp sugar
1 heaping tsp cream of tartar
1 heaping tsp baking soda
2 cups all-purpose flour
4 cups whole-wheat flour
2 cups sour milk or fresh milk mixed with
1 tbsp yogurt

Add salt, sugar, cream of tartar and baking soda to the all-purpose flour. Sift into a large mixing bowl. Add whole-wheat flour and mix thoroughly with a round-ended knife, using a lifting motion to aerate the mixture. Make a well in the center and add milk, mixing until the dough leaves the sides of the bowl clean. Knead into a ball, flatten slightly and place on a greased cookie tray. Cut a cross into the top of the loaf. Brush the top with a little milk and bake in a preheated oven, 400°F, for 40 minutes. Remove from the oven, turn loaf upside down and return to the oven for another five minutes. The loaf is done when it sounds hollow when tapped on the base. Wrap it in a slightly dampened cloth and stand on its side to cool. Cut into quarters, slice and butter generously.

Excellent with shrimp, smoked salmon or fish pâté, or at tea time with strawberry jam.

Yellow Man

INGREDIENTS
1 heaping tbsp butter
1 cup brown sugar
4 cups corn syrup
2 tbsps distilled white vinegar
1 tsp baking powder

Melt the butter in a saucepan and coat the inside of the pan with it. Add the sugar and syrup, and finally the vinegar. Stir over a low heat until the sugar and syrup have melted. Bring the mixture to a boil and simmer without stirring. Test by dropping a little into a cup of cold water to see if it sets. Add the baking powder, which will make the mixture foam up. Stir well again, pour into a greased pan and cut into squares. It may also be turned out onto a slab after the boiling process, then pulled until it becomes pale yellow in color. When it hardens it is broken into pieces with a little hammer like toffee used to be.

Right: Irish sheep and cows graze happily in this magical land of mists and leprechauns.

138

Index

Almond Tart 107

Apple Cake 112

Bacon and Egg Pie 57

Baked Custard 121

Baked Stuffed Mackerel 37

Bananas with Irish Mist 108

Barm Brack 130

Beef Braised in Guinness 66

Boiled Chicken 74

Boiled Ham and Cabbage 62

Boiled Lamb and Caper Sauce 82

Boiled Lobster 49

Boxty Pancakes 98

Braised Liver and Bacon 79

Bread and Butter Pudding 116

Broiled Trout with Almonds 35

Carrageen Moss Pudding 125

Champ 92

Colcannon 89

Country Broth 24

Crubeens 61

Curried Shrimp Salad 46

Drisheen 70

Dublin Bay Prawn Cocktail 16

Dublin Coddle 54

Dulse 94

Flummery 103

Golden Raisin Soda Bread 134

Guinness Cake 129

Irish Coffee Cake 133

Irish Rarebit 97

Irish Soda Bread 137

Irish Stew 59
Limerick Ham 65
Mackerel Rolls 45
Marinated Pork Chops 81
Mushrooms on Toast 96
Mussels in White Wine 15
Nettle Soup 23
Oaten Farls 102
Pheasant in Red Wine 77
Poached Salmon Garni 38
Potato Cakes 101
Potato Soup 20
Queen of Puddings 120
Raspberry Soufflé 122
Rhubarb Fool 115
Salmon Flan 41
Sausage Pie 69
Scallops au Gratin 28
Seafood Pancakes 44
Smoked Mackerel Pâté 19
Smoked Salmon Bisque 27
Smoked Salmon Rolls 42
Sole Surprise 33
Spiced Beef 53
Stuffed Breast of Lamb 85
Stuffed Grape Leaves 93
Stuffed Summer Squash 90
Summer Pudding 119
Tarragon Chicken 73
Tipsy Cake 111
Yellow Man 138